I will fill this journal with memories of:

HONORING
Ms. Bee

I wish you knew how I carry you with me always — everywhere I go.

~ Ranata Suzuki

If I'm having a tough day, my support system includes the following:

My parent(s) or a trusted family member:

____

My therapist or mental health provider:

____

My spiritual /or youth leader:

____

My dependable friend :

____

Others I can rely on for support include:

____

____

____

____

____

____

____

Things I've learned about myself since you passed away...

Things I've learned about myself since you passed away...

I keep myself busy with things to do, but each time I pause,
I think of you. ~ Unknown

Things I've learned about myself since you passed away...

I remember this the most about you...

The reality is that you will grieve forever. You will not "get over"
the loss of a loved one; you'll learn to live with it.

~ Elisabeth Kubler-Ross

I remember this the most about you...

I remember this the most about you...

The signs I see that make me think of you...

The signs I see that make me think of you...

____

____

____

____

____

____

____

____

____

____

____

____

____

____

____

____

____

Those we love never truly leave us. There are things that death cannot touch. ~ Jack Thorne

The signs I see that make me think of you...

This is what hurts me the most while living without you...

____

____

____

____

____

____

____

____

____

____

____

____

____

____

____

____

____

May there be comfort in knowing someone so special will never be forgotten. ~ Julie Hebert

This is what hurts me the most while living without you...

This is what hurts me the most while living without you...

I'll Always Cherish...

Use this space to add what you will always remember.

Our favorite photo together

The last things you said to me

____

Our favorite songs

____

Our favorite movies

____

Our favorite restaurants

____

Our favorite vacation

____

Our favorite joke (that only made us laugh)

____

30 Things I Can Do To Feel Better

Use this space to create a list of up to 30 activities you can engage in to feel better when you're feeling sad.

1. _______________________
2. _______________________
3. _______________________
4. _______________________
5. _______________________
6. _______________________
7. _______________________
8. _______________________
9. _______________________
10. _______________________
11. _______________________
12. _______________________
13. _______________________
14. _______________________
15. _______________________

16. _______________________
17. _______________________
18. _______________________
19. _______________________
20. _______________________
21. _______________________
22. _______________________
23. _______________________
24. _______________________
25. _______________________
26. _______________________
27. _______________________
28. _______________________
29. _______________________
30. _______________________

10 words That Describe You

Add Your Favorite Photo of Your Loved One

Use this space to write down 10 words that describe your loved one. You may add words that are serious, funny, or loving.

1. ___________________________________

2. ___________________________________

3. ___________________________________

4. ___________________________________

5. ___________________________________

6. ___________________________________

7. ___________________________________

8. ___________________________________

9. ___________________________________

10. ___________________________________

Date: ____ / ____ / ____

If I feel sad and need emotional support today, I will contact:

____

If you were here now... _________________________

____

____

My first thoughts of today... ____________________

____

My school/teachers/friends can help me during this time by... _______________________

____

____

What helps me remember you... ____

____

____

I'm really missing this about you... ____

____

Sometimes it feels like I'm the only one that remembers you; that makes me... _________

____

____

Every time is see/hear this: ____ I think of you.

What I would tell you about my day... ____

____

The hardest part of my day is... ____

____

Today I'm really missing... ____

____

I find comfort when... ____

____

Date: /   /

If I feel sad and need emotional support today, I will contact:

____

If you were here now... _______________________________

____

____

My first thoughts of today... __________________________

____

My school/teachers/friends can help me during this time by... ______________

____

____

What helps me remember you... _________________________________

____

____

I'm really missing this about you... ______________________________

____

Sometimes it feels like I'm the only one that remembers you; that makes me... _______

____

____

Every time is see/hear this: _________________________ I think of you.

What I would tell you about my day... _____________________________

____

The hardest part of my day is... ________________________________

____

Today I'm really missing... ___________________________________

____

I find comfort when... _______________________________________

____

Date: /   /

If I feel sad and need emotional support today, I will contact:

____

If you were here now... _________________________

____

____

My first thoughts of today... ____________________

____

<table>
<tr><td>Today I:</td></tr>
<tr><td>☐ Feel neutral/okay</td></tr>
<tr><td>☐ Feel supported</td></tr>
<tr><td>☐ Feel brokenhearted</td></tr>
<tr><td>☐ Feel misunderstood</td></tr>
<tr><td>☐ Feel like crying</td></tr>
<tr><td>☐ Feel lonely</td></tr>
<tr><td>☐ Feel angry</td></tr>
<tr><td>☐ Feel tired</td></tr>
<tr><td>☐ Feel sad</td></tr>
</table>

My school/teachers/friends can help me during this time by... ____________________

____

____

What helps me remember you... __________________

____

____

I'm really missing this about you... ______________

____

Sometimes it feels like I'm the only one that remembers you; that makes me... ________

____

____

Every time is see/hear this: ______________________ I think of you.

What I would tell you about my day... _____________

____

The hardest part of my day is... _________________

____

Today I'm really missing... _____________________

____

I find comfort when... __________________________

____

Date: / /

If I feel sad and need emotional support today, I will contact:

____

If you were here now... __________________________

____

____

My first thoughts of today... __________________

My school/teachers/friends can help me during this time by... __________________

____

____

What helps me remember you... ____

____

____

I'm really missing this about you... ____________________________________

____

Sometimes it feels like I'm the only one that remembers you; that makes me... ________

____

____

Every time is see/hear this: _________________________________ I think of you.

What I would tell you about my day... ___________________________________

____

The hardest part of my day is... ____

____

Today I'm really missing... ____

____

I find comfort when... ____

____

Date: /   /

If I feel sad and need emotional support today, I will contact:

____

If you were here now... _______________________________

____

____

My first thoughts of today... _____________________________

____

My school/teachers/friends can help me during this time by... __________________

____

____

What helps me remember you... _______________________________

____

____

I'm really missing this about you... _______________________________

____

Sometimes it feels like I'm the only one that remembers you; that makes me... ________

____

____

Every time is see/hear this: _________________________________ I think of you.

What I would tell you about my day... _______________________________

____

The hardest part of my day is... _______________________________

____

Today I'm really missing... _______________________________

____

I find comfort when... _______________________________

____

Date: /   /

If I feel sad and need emotional support today, I will contact:

____

If you were here now... _______________________________________

____

____

My first thoughts of today... _________________________________

____

My school/teachers/friends can help me during this time by... _______________

____

____

What helps me remember you... _________________________________

____

____

I'm really missing this about you... ____________________________

____

Sometimes it feels like I'm the only one that remembers you; that makes me... ________

____

____

Every time is see/hear this: _________________________ I think of you.

What I would tell you about my day... ___________________________

____

The hardest part of my day is... _______________________________

____

Today I'm really missing... ___________________________________

____

I find comfort when... _______________________________________

____

Date: ___ / ___ / ___

If I feel sad and need emotional support today, I will contact:

____

If you were here now... _________________________________

____

____

My first thoughts of today... ____________________________

____

My school/teachers/friends can help me during this time by... _______________

____

____

What helps me remember you... __________________________________

____

____

I'm really missing this about you... _______________________________

____

Sometimes it feels like I'm the only one that remembers you; that makes me... ________

____

____

Every time is see/hear this: ______________________________ I think of you.

What I would tell you about my day... _____________________________

____

The hardest part of my day is... _________________________________

____

Today I'm really missing... ____________________________________

____

I find comfort when... ____

____

Date: / /

If I feel sad and need emotional support today, I will contact:

____

If you were here now... ___________________________

____

____

My first thoughts of today... ___________________

____

My school/teachers/friends can help me during this time by... ___________________

____

____

What helps me remember you... ____

____

____

I'm really missing this about you... ____

____

Sometimes it feels like I'm the only one that remembers you; that makes me... _______

____

____

Every time is see/hear this: _______________________________ I think of you.

What I would tell you about my day... ___________________________________

____

The hardest part of my day is... ____

____

Today I'm really missing... ____

____

I find comfort when... ____

____

$\mathcal{Date}$:   /   /

If I feel sad and need emotional support today, I will contact:

____

If you were here now... _________________________

____

____

My first thoughts of today... ____________________

____

My school/teachers/friends can help me during this time by... _______________________

____

____

What helps me remember you... ____

____

____

I'm really missing this about you... _______________________________________

____

Sometimes it feels like I'm the only one that remembers you; that makes me... ________

____

____

Every time is see/hear this: _________________________________ I think of you.

What I would tell you about my day... _____________________________________

____

The hardest part of my day is... ____

____

Today I'm really missing... ____

____

I find comfort when... ____

____

Date: /   /

<table>
<tr><td>

If I feel sad and need emotional support today, I will contact:

____

If you were here now... _______________________

____

____

My first thoughts of today... _________________

</td><td>

Today I:

☐ Feel neutral/okay
☐ Feel supported
☐ Feel brokenhearted
☐ Feel misunderstood
☐ Feel like crying
☐ Feel lonely
☐ Feel angry
☐ Feel tired
☐ Feel sad

</td></tr>
</table>

____

My school/teachers/friends can help me during this time by... _______________

____

____

What helps me remember you... _______________________________________

____

____

I'm really missing this about you... _________________________________

____

Sometimes it feels like I'm the only one that remembers you; that makes me... ________

____

____

Every time is see/hear this: _____________________________ I think of you.

What I would tell you about my day... _______________________________

____

The hardest part of my day is... ___________________________________

____

Today I'm really missing... _______________________________________

____

I find comfort when... ____

____

Date: / /

If I feel sad and need emotional support today, I will contact:

____

If you were here now... _______________________________

____

____

My first thoughts of today... _______________________

____

My school/teachers/friends can help me during this time by... _______________________

____

____

What helps me remember you... ____

____

____

I'm really missing this about you... ____

____

Sometimes it feels like I'm the only one that remembers you; that makes me... _________

____

____

Every time is see/hear this: _________________________________ I think of you.

What I would tell you about my day... _______________________________________

____

The hardest part of my day is... _______________________________________

____

Today I'm really missing... _______________________________________

____

I find comfort when... _______________________________________

____

$\mathcal{D}ate$:   /   /

If I feel sad and need emotional support today, I will contact:

____

If you were here now... ___________________________

____

____

My first thoughts of today... _____________________

____

<table>
<tr><td>Today I:</td></tr>
<tr><td>☐ Feel neutral/okay</td></tr>
<tr><td>☐ Feel supported</td></tr>
<tr><td>☐ Feel brokenhearted</td></tr>
<tr><td>☐ Feel misunderstood</td></tr>
<tr><td>☐ Feel like crying</td></tr>
<tr><td>☐ Feel lonely</td></tr>
<tr><td>☐ Feel angry</td></tr>
<tr><td>☐ Feel tired</td></tr>
<tr><td>☐ Feel sad</td></tr>
</table>

My school/teachers/friends can help me during this time by... ___________________

____

____

What helps me remember you... ____________________________________

____

____

I'm really missing this about you... ______________________________

____

Sometimes it feels like I'm the only one that remembers you; that makes me... ________

____

____

Every time is see/hear this: _________________________ I think of you.

What I would tell you about my day... _____________________________

____

The hardest part of my day is... __________________________________

____

Today I'm really missing... _______________________________________

____

I find comfort when... ____

____

Date: / /

If I feel sad and need emotional support today, I will contact:

____

If you were here now... _________________________

____

____

My first thoughts of today... ____________________

____

My school/teachers/friends can help me during this time by... ____________________

____

____

What helps me remember you... ____

____

____

I'm really missing this about you... ______________________________________

____

Sometimes it feels like I'm the only one that remembers you; that makes me... ________

____

____

Every time is see/hear this: ___________________________________ I think of you.

What I would tell you about my day... _____________________________________

____

The hardest part of my day is... ____

____

Today I'm really missing... ____

____

I find comfort when... ____

____

Date: /   /

If I feel sad and need emotional support today, I will contact:

____

If you were here now... ____________________

____

____

My first thoughts of today... ______________

____

My school/teachers/friends can help me during this time by... ____________________

____

____

What helps me remember you... ____________________

____

____

I'm really missing this about you... ____________________

____

Sometimes it feels like I'm the only one that remembers you; that makes me... ________

____

____

Every time is see/hear this: _________________________ I think of you.

What I would tell you about my day... ____________________

____

The hardest part of my day is... ____________________

____

Today I'm really missing... ____________________

____

I find comfort when... ____________________

____

Date: /   /

If I feel sad and need emotional support today, I will contact:

____

If you were here now... _______________________________

____

____

My first thoughts of today... __________________________

____

My school/teachers/friends can help me during this time by... _______________

____

____

What helps me remember you... _________________________

____

____

I'm really missing this about you... ____________________

____

Sometimes it feels like I'm the only one that remembers you; that makes me... ________

____

____

Every time is see/hear this: ____________________________ I think of you.

What I would tell you about my day... ___________________

____

The hardest part of my day is... ________________________

____

Today I'm really missing... ____________________________

____

I find comfort when... _________________________________

____

$\mathcal{D}ate$:   /   /

If I feel sad and need emotional support today, I will contact:

____

If you were here now... _______________________________

____

____

My first thoughts of today... ___________________________

____

<table>
<tr><td>Today I:</td></tr>
<tr><td>☐ Feel neutral/okay</td></tr>
<tr><td>☐ Feel supported</td></tr>
<tr><td>☐ Feel brokenhearted</td></tr>
<tr><td>☐ Feel misunderstood</td></tr>
<tr><td>☐ Feel like crying</td></tr>
<tr><td>☐ Feel lonely</td></tr>
<tr><td>☐ Feel angry</td></tr>
<tr><td>☐ Feel tired</td></tr>
<tr><td>☐ Feel sad</td></tr>
</table>

My school/teachers/friends can help me during this time by... ________________

____

____

What helps me remember you... _________________________________

____

____

I'm really missing this about you... _______________________________

____

Sometimes it feels like I'm the only one that remembers you; that makes me... ________

____

____

Every time is see/hear this: _________________________ I think of you.

What I would tell you about my day... ____________________________

____

The hardest part of my day is... ________________________________

____

Today I'm really missing... ___________________________________

____

I find comfort when... _______________________________________

____

Date: /   /

If I feel sad and need emotional support today, I will contact:

____

If you were here now... _________________________

____

____

My first thoughts of today... ____________________

____

My school/teachers/friends can help me during this time by... _______________

____

____

What helps me remember you... ___________________________________

____

____

I'm really missing this about you... _______________________________

____

Sometimes it feels like I'm the only one that remembers you; that makes me... _______

____

____

Every time is see/hear this: _________________________________ I think of you.

What I would tell you about my day... ______________________________

____

The hardest part of my day is... _________________________________

____

Today I'm really missing... ____________________________________

____

I find comfort when... _______________________________________

____

Date: ___ / ___ / ___

If I feel sad and need emotional support today, I will contact:

____

If you were here now... _________________________________

____

____

My first thoughts of today... _____________________________

____

My school/teachers/friends can help me during this time by... _______________

____

____

What helps me remember you... ___________________________________

____

____

I'm really missing this about you... ________________________________

____

Sometimes it feels like I'm the only one that remembers you; that makes me... _________

____

____

Every time is see/hear this: ___________________________ I think of you.

What I would tell you about my day... _______________________________

____

The hardest part of my day is... __________________________________

____

Today I'm really missing... _____________________________________

____

I find comfort when... ____

____

Date: / /

If I feel sad and need emotional support today, I will contact:

____

If you were here now... __________________________

____

____

My first thoughts of today... ___________________

____

My school/teachers/friends can help me during this time by... ________________

____

____

What helps me remember you... _________________________________

____

____

I'm really missing this about you... __________________________________

____

Sometimes it feels like I'm the only one that remembers you; that makes me... ________

____

____

Every time is see/hear this: ________________________________ I think of you.

What I would tell you about my day... _______________________________

____

The hardest part of my day is... ___________________________________

____

Today I'm really missing... _______________________________________

____

I find comfort when... ____

____

Date: __ / __ / __

If I feel sad and need emotional support today, I will contact:

____

If you were here now... ___________________________

____

____

My first thoughts of today... ______________________

____

My school/teachers/friends can help me during this time by... _______________

____

____

What helps me remember you... ____________________________________

____

____

I'm really missing this about you... _________________________________

____

Sometimes it feels like I'm the only one that remembers you; that makes me... ________

____

____

Every time is see/hear this: _________________________________ I think of you.

What I would tell you about my day... ________________________________

____

The hardest part of my day is... ____________________________________

____

Today I'm really missing... _______________________________________

____

I find comfort when... ____

____

Date: / /

If I feel sad and need emotional support today, I will contact:

____

If you were here now... _______________________________

____

____

My first thoughts of today... _________________________

____

My school/teachers/friends can help me during this time by... _______________________

____

____

What helps me remember you... _______________________________

____

____

I'm really missing this about you... ______________________________

____

Sometimes it feels like I'm the only one that remembers you; that makes me... _______

____

____

Every time is see/hear this: _________________________________ I think of you.

What I would tell you about my day... _______________________________

____

The hardest part of my day is... ___________________________________

____

Today I'm really missing... _______________________________________

____

I find comfort when... ____

____

Date: ___ / ___ / ___

If I feel sad and need emotional support today, I will contact:

____

If you were here now... _______________________________

____

____

My first thoughts of today... _______________________

____

My school/teachers/friends can help me during this time by... ___________________

____

____

What helps me remember you... _________________________________

____

____

I'm really missing this about you... _______________________________

____

Sometimes it feels like I'm the only one that remembers you; that makes me... _______

____

____

Every time is see/hear this: _________________________________ I think of you.

What I would tell you about my day... _______________________________

____

The hardest part of my day is... _________________________________

____

Today I'm really missing... _________________________________

____

I find comfort when... _________________________________

____

Date: /   /

If I feel sad and need emotional support today, I will contact:

____

If you were here now... _______________________

____

____

My first thoughts of today... _________________

My school/teachers/friends can help me during this time by... _______________________

____

____

What helps me remember you... ____

____

____

I'm really missing this about you... ____

____

Sometimes it feels like I'm the only one that remembers you; that makes me... ________

____

____

Every time is see/hear this: ______________________________________ I think of you.

What I would tell you about my day... ____

____

The hardest part of my day is... ____

____

Today I'm really missing... ____

____

I find comfort when... ____

____

Date: /   /

If I feel sad and need emotional support today, I will contact:

____

If you were here now... _______________________

____

____

My first thoughts of today... __________________

____

<table>
<tr><td>Today I:</td></tr>
<tr><td>☐ Feel neutral/okay</td></tr>
<tr><td>☐ Feel supported</td></tr>
<tr><td>☐ Feel brokenhearted</td></tr>
<tr><td>☐ Feel misunderstood</td></tr>
<tr><td>☐ Feel like crying</td></tr>
<tr><td>☐ Feel lonely</td></tr>
<tr><td>☐ Feel angry</td></tr>
<tr><td>☐ Feel tired</td></tr>
<tr><td>☐ Feel sad</td></tr>
</table>

My school/teachers/friends can help me during this time by... ____________________

____

____

What helps me remember you... ____

____

____

I'm really missing this about you... ____________________________________

____

Sometimes it feels like I'm the only one that remembers you; that makes me... _______

____

____

Every time is see/hear this: _______________________________ I think of you.

What I would tell you about my day... ___________________________________

____

The hardest part of my day is... _______________________________________

____

Today I'm really missing... ____

____

I find comfort when... ____

____

Date: ___ / ___ / ___

If I feel sad and need emotional support today, I will contact:

____

If you were here now... _______________________________

____

____

My first thoughts of today... __________________________

____

My school/teachers/friends can help me during this time by... _________________

____

____

What helps me remember you... _________________________________

____

____

I'm really missing this about you... _______________________________

____

Sometimes it feels like I'm the only one that remembers you; that makes me... _______

____

____

Every time is see/hear this: ___________________________ I think of you.

What I would tell you about my day... _____________________________

____

The hardest part of my day is... ________________________________

____

Today I'm really missing... ___________________________________

____

I find comfort when... ______________________________________

____

Date: / /

If I feel sad and need emotional support today, I will contact:

____

If you were here now... ___________________________

____

____

My first thoughts of today... ___________________________

____

My school/teachers/friends can help me during this time by... ___________________

____

____

What helps me remember you... ___________________________________

____

____

I'm really missing this about you... ___________________________________

____

Sometimes it feels like I'm the only one that remembers you; that makes me... _______

____

____

Every time is see/hear this: _____________________________ I think of you.

What I would tell you about my day... _______________________________

____

The hardest part of my day is... _________________________________

____

Today I'm really missing... _____________________________________

____

I find comfort when... ____

____

If I feel sad and need emotional support today, I will contact:

____

If you were here now... _______________________________

____

____

My first thoughts of today... _______________________

____

My school/teachers/friends can help me during this time by... _______________________

____

____

What helps me remember you... _______________________________

____

____

I'm really missing this about you... _______________________________

____

Sometimes it feels like I'm the only one that remembers you; that makes me... _______

____

____

Every time is see/hear this: _______________________________ I think of you.

What I would tell you about my day... _______________________________

____

The hardest part of my day is... _______________________________

____

Today I'm really missing... _______________________________

____

I find comfort when... _______________________________

____

Date: /   /

If I feel sad and need emotional support today, I will contact:

____

If you were here now... _______________________________

____

____

My first thoughts of today... _______________________

____

My school/teachers/friends can help me during this time by... ___________________

____

____

What helps me remember you... _________________________________

____

____

I'm really missing this about you... ______________________________

____

Sometimes it feels like I'm the only one that remembers you; that makes me... _______

____

____

Every time is see/hear this: ___________________________ I think of you.

What I would tell you about my day... ______________________________

____

The hardest part of my day is... _________________________________

____

Today I'm really missing... ____________________________________

____

I find comfort when... ____

____

Date: / /

If I feel sad and need emotional support today, I will contact:

____

If you were here now... ______________________

____

____

My first thoughts of today... __________________

____

My school/teachers/friends can help me during this time by... ______________

____

____

What helps me remember you... ________________________________

____

____

I'm really missing this about you... __________________________________

____

Sometimes it feels like I'm the only one that remembers you; that makes me... ________

____

____

Every time is see/hear this: ________________________________ I think of you.

What I would tell you about my day... ________________________________

____

The hardest part of my day is... ________________________________

____

Today I'm really missing... ________________________________

____

I find comfort when... ________________________________

____

Date: /   /

If I feel sad and need emotional support today, I will contact:

____

If you were here now... _________________________

____

____

My first thoughts of today... ___________________

My school/teachers/friends can help me during this time by... _________________________

____

____

What helps me remember you... ____

____

____

I'm really missing this about you... ____

____

Sometimes it feels like I'm the only one that remembers you; that makes me... _________

____

____

Every time is see/hear this: _________________________________ I think of you.

What I would tell you about my day... ____

____

The hardest part of my day is... ____

____

Today I'm really missing... ____

____

I find comfort when... ____

____

Date: ___ / ___ / ___

If I feel sad and need emotional support today, I will contact:

____

If you were here now... _________________________

____

____

My first thoughts of today... _____________________

____

My school/teachers/friends can help me during this time by... _______________

____

____

What helps me remember you... __________________________________

____

____

I'm really missing this about you... _________________________________

____

Sometimes it feels like I'm the only one that remembers you; that makes me... _______

____

____

Every time is see/hear this: _____________________________ I think of you.

What I would tell you about my day... _______________________________

____

The hardest part of my day is... __________________________________

____

Today I'm really missing... ______________________________________

____

I find comfort when... ____

____

Date: _____ / _____ / _____

If I feel sad and need emotional support today, I will contact:

____

If you were here now... ____________________________

____

____

My first thoughts of today... ______________________

____

My school/teachers/friends can help me during this time by... ____________________

____

____

What helps me remember you... _____________________________________

____

____

I'm really missing this about you... ________________________________

____

Sometimes it feels like I'm the only one that remembers you; that makes me... ________

____

____

Every time is see/hear this: ___________________________________ I think of you.

What I would tell you about my day... _______________________________

____

The hardest part of my day is... ___________________________________

____

Today I'm really missing... _______________________________________

____

I find comfort when... ____

____

$Date$:   /   /

If I feel sad and need emotional support today, I will contact:

____

If you were here now... _______________________________

____

____

My first thoughts of today... _______________________

____

My school/teachers/friends can help me during this time by... _______________

____

____

What helps me remember you... _________________________________

____

____

I'm really missing this about you... ___________________________________

____

Sometimes it feels like I'm the only one that remembers you; that makes me... _________

____

____

Every time is see/hear this: ______________________________ I think of you.

What I would tell you about my day... _______________________________

____

The hardest part of my day is... ____________________________________

____

Today I'm really missing... ____

____

I find comfort when... ____

____

Date: ____ / ____ / ____

If I feel sad and need emotional support today, I will contact:

____

If you were here now... _______________________________

____

____

My first thoughts of today... _______________________

____

My school/teachers/friends can help me during this time by... _______________

____

____

What helps me remember you... ___________________________________

____

____

I'm really missing this about you... _________________________________

____

Sometimes it feels like I'm the only one that remembers you; that makes me... ________

____

____

Every time is see/hear this: _______________________________ I think of you.

What I would tell you about my day... _______________________________

____

The hardest part of my day is... ___________________________________

____

Today I'm really missing... _______________________________________

____

I find comfort when... ____

____

Date: ___ / ___ / ___

<table>
<tr><td>

If I feel sad and need emotional support today, I will contact:

____

If you were here now... _______________________

____

____

My first thoughts of today... _________________

____

</td><td>

Today I:

☐ Feel neutral/okay
☐ Feel supported
☐ Feel brokenhearted
☐ Feel misunderstood
☐ Feel like crying
☐ Feel lonely
☐ Feel angry
☐ Feel tired
☐ Feel sad

</td></tr>
</table>

My school/teachers/friends can help me during this time by... _______________________

____

____

What helps me remember you... _____________________________________

____

____

I'm really missing this about you... ___________________________________

____

Sometimes it feels like I'm the only one that remembers you; that makes me... ________

____

____

Every time is see/hear this: ________________________________ I think of you.

What I would tell you about my day... _________________________________

____

The hardest part of my day is... _____________________________________

____

Today I'm really missing... ____

____

I find comfort when... ____

____

Date: /   /

If I feel sad and need emotional support today, I will contact:

____

If you were here now... _______________________

____

____

My first thoughts of today... ___________________

My school/teachers/friends can help me during this time by... _______________________

____

____

What helps me remember you... _______________________

____

____

I'm really missing this about you... _______________________

____

Sometimes it feels like I'm the only one that remembers you; that makes me... _________

____

____

Every time is see/hear this: _______________________ I think of you.

What I would tell you about my day... _______________________

____

The hardest part of my day is... _______________________

____

Today I'm really missing... _______________________

____

I find comfort when... _______________________

____

Date: ___ / ___ / ___

If I feel sad and need emotional support today, I will contact:

____

If you were here now... _______________________________

____

____

My first thoughts of today... _______________________________

____

My school/teachers/friends can help me during this time by... __________________

____

____

What helps me remember you... _______________________________________

____

____

I'm really missing this about you... _______________________________________

____

Sometimes it feels like I'm the only one that remembers you; that makes me... _________

____

____

Every time is see/hear this: _______________________________ I think of you.

What I would tell you about my day... _______________________________________

____

The hardest part of my day is... _______________________________________

____

Today I'm really missing... _______________________________________

____

I find comfort when... _______________________________________

____

Date: /   /

If I feel sad and need emotional support today, I will contact:

____

If you were here now... _______________________________

____

____

My first thoughts of today... ___________________________

____

<table>
<tr><td>Today I:</td></tr>
<tr><td>☐ Feel neutral/okay</td></tr>
<tr><td>☐ Feel supported</td></tr>
<tr><td>☐ Feel brokenhearted</td></tr>
<tr><td>☐ Feel misunderstood</td></tr>
<tr><td>☐ Feel like crying</td></tr>
<tr><td>☐ Feel lonely</td></tr>
<tr><td>☐ Feel angry</td></tr>
<tr><td>☐ Feel tired</td></tr>
<tr><td>☐ Feel sad</td></tr>
</table>

My school/teachers/friends can help me during this time by... _______________

____

____

What helps me remember you... _________________________________

____

____

I'm really missing this about you... _______________________________

____

Sometimes it feels like I'm the only one that remembers you; that makes me... ________

____

____

Every time is see/hear this: ________________________________ I think of you.

What I would tell you about my day... _____________________________

____

The hardest part of my day is... _________________________________

____

Today I'm really missing... ____________________________________

____

I find comfort when... _______________________________________

____

Date: / /

If I feel sad and need emotional support today, I will contact:

____

If you were here now... _________________________

____

____

My first thoughts of today... ____________________

____

My school/teachers/friends can help me during this time by... _______________

____

____

What helps me remember you... ___________________________________

____

____

I'm really missing this about you... ___________________________________

____

Sometimes it feels like I'm the only one that remembers you; that makes me... ________

____

____

Every time is see/hear this: ________________________________ I think of you.

What I would tell you about my day... _______________________________

____

The hardest part of my day is... ___________________________________

____

Today I'm really missing... _______________________________________

____

I find comfort when... ____

____

Date: /   /

If I feel sad and need emotional support today, I will contact:

____

If you were here now... _______________________________

____

____

My first thoughts of today... ___________________________

____

My school/teachers/friends can help me during this time by... _______________________

____

____

What helps me remember you... ____

____

____

I'm really missing this about you... ____

____

Sometimes it feels like I'm the only one that remembers you; that makes me... _________

____

____

Every time is see/hear this: ___________________________________ I think of you.

What I would tell you about my day... ____

____

The hardest part of my day is... ____

____

Today I'm really missing... ____

____

I find comfort when... ____

____

Date: ___ / ___ / ___

If I feel sad and need emotional support today, I will contact:

____

If you were here now... ____________________________

____

____

My first thoughts of today... ____________________

____

My school/teachers/friends can help me during this time by... ____________________

____

____

What helps me remember you... ____________________

____

____

I'm really missing this about you... ____________________

____

Sometimes it feels like I'm the only one that remembers you; that makes me... ________

____

____

Every time is see/hear this: ____________________ I think of you.

What I would tell you about my day... ____________________

____

The hardest part of my day is... ____________________

____

Today I'm really missing... ____________________

____

I find comfort when... ____________________

____

$\mathcal{D}$ate: /   /

If I feel sad and need emotional support today, I will contact:

____

If you were here now... _______________________________

____

____

My first thoughts of today... _______________________

____

My school/teachers/friends can help me during this time by... _______________________

____

____

What helps me remember you... _______________________________

____

____

I'm really missing this about you... _______________________________

____

Sometimes it feels like I'm the only one that remembers you; that makes me... _________

____

____

Every time is see/hear this: _______________________________ I think of you.

What I would tell you about my day... _______________________________

____

The hardest part of my day is... _______________________________

____

Today I'm really missing... _______________________________

____

I find comfort when... _______________________________

____

Date: / /

If I feel sad and need emotional support today, I will contact:

____

If you were here now... _______________________

____

____

My first thoughts of today... _________________

____

My school/teachers/friends can help me during this time by... _______________________

____

____

What helps me remember you... _______________________

____

____

I'm really missing this about you... _______________________

____

Sometimes it feels like I'm the only one that remembers you; that makes me... ________

____

____

Every time is see/hear this: _____________________________ I think of you.

What I would tell you about my day... _______________________

____

The hardest part of my day is... _______________________

____

Today I'm really missing... _______________________

____

I find comfort when... _______________________

____

Date: ___ / ___ / ___

If I feel sad and need emotional support today, I will contact:

____

If you were here now... _______________________________

____

____

My first thoughts of today... ___________________________

____

My school/teachers/friends can help me during this time by... _______________

____

____

What helps me remember you... _________________________________

____

____

I'm really missing this about you... _______________________________

____

Sometimes it feels like I'm the only one that remembers you; that makes me... _______

____

____

Every time is see/hear this: ______________________________ I think of you.

What I would tell you about my day... _____________________________

____

The hardest part of my day is... ________________________________

____

Today I'm really missing... ___________________________________

____

I find comfort when... _______________________________________

____

Date: /   /

If I feel sad and need emotional support today, I will contact:

____

If you were here now... _________________________

____

____

My first thoughts of today... ____________________

____

<table>
<tr><td>Today I:</td></tr>
<tr><td>☐ Feel neutral/okay</td></tr>
<tr><td>☐ Feel supported</td></tr>
<tr><td>☐ Feel brokenhearted</td></tr>
<tr><td>☐ Feel misunderstood</td></tr>
<tr><td>☐ Feel like crying</td></tr>
<tr><td>☐ Feel lonely</td></tr>
<tr><td>☐ Feel angry</td></tr>
<tr><td>☐ Feel tired</td></tr>
<tr><td>☐ Feel sad</td></tr>
</table>

My school/teachers/friends can help me during this time by... _________________

____

____

What helps me remember you... __________________

____

____

I'm really missing this about you... ______________

____

Sometimes it feels like I'm the only one that remembers you; that makes me... _______

____

____

Every time is see/hear this: _________________________ I think of you.

What I would tell you about my day... ____________

____

The hardest part of my day is... _________________

____

Today I'm really missing... _____________________

____

I find comfort when... _________________________

____

Date: ___ / ___ / ___

If I feel sad and need emotional support today, I will contact:

____

If you were here now... _______________________

____

____

My first thoughts of today... _________________

____

My school/teachers/friends can help me during this time by... _______________________

____

____

What helps me remember you... _______________________

____

____

I'm really missing this about you... _______________________

____

Sometimes it feels like I'm the only one that remembers you; that makes me... _______

____

____

Every time is see/hear this: _______________________ I think of you.

What I would tell you about my day... _______________________

____

The hardest part of my day is... _______________________

____

Today I'm really missing... _______________________

____

I find comfort when... _______________________

____

Date: / /

If I feel sad and need emotional support today, I will contact:

____

If you were here now... _________________________________

____

____

My first thoughts of today... _____________________________

____

My school/teachers/friends can help me during this time by... ___________________

____

____

What helps me remember you... ____

____

____

I'm really missing this about you... ____

____

Sometimes it feels like I'm the only one that remembers you; that makes me... _______

____

____

Every time is see/hear this: _________________________________ I think of you.

What I would tell you about my day... ______________________________________

____

The hardest part of my day is... ____

____

Today I'm really missing... ____

____

I find comfort when... ____

____

If I feel sad and need emotional support today, I will contact:

____

If you were here now... _______________________________

____

____

My first thoughts of today... ____________________________

____

<table>
<tr><td>Today I:</td></tr>
<tr><td>☐ Feel neutral/okay</td></tr>
<tr><td>☐ Feel supported</td></tr>
<tr><td>☐ Feel brokenhearted</td></tr>
<tr><td>☐ Feel misunderstood</td></tr>
<tr><td>☐ Feel like crying</td></tr>
<tr><td>☐ Feel lonely</td></tr>
<tr><td>☐ Feel angry</td></tr>
<tr><td>☐ Feel tired</td></tr>
<tr><td>☐ Feel sad</td></tr>
</table>

My school/teachers/friends can help me during this time by... ____________________

____

____

What helps me remember you... __________________________________

____

____

I'm really missing this about you... _________________________________

____

Sometimes it feels like I'm the only one that remembers you; that makes me... _________

____

____

Every time is see/hear this: _________________________________ I think of you.

What I would tell you about my day... _______________________________

____

The hardest part of my day is... ___________________________________

____

Today I'm really missing... ______________________________________

____

I find comfort when... ____

____

Date: ___ / ___ / ___

If I feel sad and need emotional support today, I will contact:

____

If you were here now... _______________________________

____

____

My first thoughts of today... _________________________

____

My school/teachers/friends can help me during this time by... _______________

____

____

What helps me remember you... ________________________________

____

____

I'm really missing this about you... ______________________________

____

Sometimes it feels like I'm the only one that remembers you; that makes me... ________

____

____

Every time is see/hear this: ____________________________ I think of you.

What I would tell you about my day... ____________________________

____

The hardest part of my day is... ________________________________

____

Today I'm really missing... ___________________________________

____

I find comfort when... ______________________________________

____

Date: / /

If I feel sad and need emotional support today, I will contact:

____

If you were here now... _______________________________

____

____

My first thoughts of today... _______________________

My school/teachers/friends can help me during this time by... _______________________

____

____

What helps me remember you... ____

____

____

I'm really missing this about you... ____

____

Sometimes it feels like I'm the only one that remembers you; that makes me... ________

____

____

Every time is see/hear this: _______________________________ I think of you.

What I would tell you about my day... _______________________________________

____

The hardest part of my day is... _______________________________________

____

Today I'm really missing... _______________________________________

____

I find comfort when... _______________________________________

____

Date: /   /

If I feel sad and need emotional support today, I will contact:

____

If you were here now... _________________________

____

____

My first thoughts of today... ____________________

____

My school/teachers/friends can help me during this time by... __________________

____

____

What helps me remember you... ____

____

____

I'm really missing this about you... ______________________________________

____

Sometimes it feels like I'm the only one that remembers you; that makes me... _______

____

____

Every time is see/hear this: _____________________________ I think of you.

What I would tell you about my day... ____________________________________

____

The hardest part of my day is... ____

____

Today I'm really missing... ____

____

I find comfort when... ____

____

Date: /   /

If I feel sad and need emotional support today, I will contact:

____

If you were here now... ___________________________________

____

____

My first thoughts of today... _________________________________

____

My school/teachers/friends can help me during this time by... _______________________

____

____

What helps me remember you... ____

____

____

I'm really missing this about you... _____________________________________

____

Sometimes it feels like I'm the only one that remembers you; that makes me... _______

____

____

Every time is see/hear this: _________________________________ I think of you.

What I would tell you about my day... __________________________________

____

The hardest part of my day is... _______________________________________

____

Today I'm really missing... ____

____

I find comfort when... ____

____

Date: / /

If I feel sad and need emotional support today, I will contact:

____

If you were here now... _______________________________

____

____

My first thoughts of today... _______________________

My school/teachers/friends can help me during this time by... _______________________

____

____

What helps me remember you... _______________________________________

____

____

I'm really missing this about you... _______________________________________

____

Sometimes it feels like I'm the only one that remembers you; that makes me... _______

____

____

Every time is see/hear this: _______________________________ I think of you.

What I would tell you about my day... _______________________________________

____

The hardest part of my day is... _______________________________________

____

Today I'm really missing... _______________________________________

____

I find comfort when... _______________________________________

____

Date: /   /

If I feel sad and need emotional support today, I will contact:

____

If you were here now... ________________________________

____

____

My first thoughts of today... ____________________________

____

My school/teachers/friends can help me during this time by... ____________________

____

____

What helps me remember you... __________________________________

____

____

I'm really missing this about you... ______________________________

____

Sometimes it feels like I'm the only one that remembers you; that makes me... ________

____

____

Every time is see/hear this: _________________________ I think of you.

What I would tell you about my day... ______________________________

____

The hardest part of my day is... __________________________________

____

Today I'm really missing... ______________________________________

____

I find comfort when... ____

____

Date: / /

If I feel sad and need emotional support today, I will contact:

____

If you were here now... ______________________________

____

____

My first thoughts of today... __________________________

____

My school/teachers/friends can help me during this time by... ______________________

____

____

What helps me remember you... ____

____

____

I'm really missing this about you... ____

____

Sometimes it feels like I'm the only one that remembers you; that makes me... ________

____

____

Every time is see/hear this: _________________________________ I think of you.

What I would tell you about my day... ____

____

The hardest part of my day is... ____

____

Today I'm really missing... ____

____

I find comfort when... ____

____

Date: ___/___/___

If I feel sad and need emotional support today, I will contact:

____

If you were here now... _______________________

____

____

My first thoughts of today... _________________

____

Today I:

☐ Feel neutral/okay

☐ Feel supported

☐ Feel brokenhearted

☐ Feel misunderstood

☐ Feel like crying

☐ Feel lonely

☐ Feel angry

☐ Feel tired

☐ Feel sad

My school/teachers/friends can help me during this time by... _______________________

____

____

What helps me remember you... _______________________

____

____

I'm really missing this about you... _______________________

____

Sometimes it feels like I'm the only one that remembers you; that makes me... _______

____

____

Every time is see/hear this: _______________________ I think of you.

What I would tell you about my day... _______________________

____

The hardest part of my day is... _______________________

____

Today I'm really missing... _______________________

____

I find comfort when... _______________________

____

Date: / /

If I feel sad and need emotional support today, I will contact:

____

If you were here now... _______________________________

____

____

My first thoughts of today... _______________________

____

My school/teachers/friends can help me during this time by... _______________

____

____

What helps me remember you... _______________________

____

____

I'm really missing this about you... _______________________

____

Sometimes it feels like I'm the only one that remembers you; that makes me... _______

____

____

Every time is see/hear this: _________________________ I think of you.

What I would tell you about my day... _______________________

____

The hardest part of my day is... _______________________

____

Today I'm really missing... _______________________

____

I find comfort when... _______________________

____

$\mathcal{D}ate$:   /   /

If I feel sad and need emotional support today, I will contact:

____

If you were here now... _______________________________

____

____

My first thoughts of today... _______________________

____

My school/teachers/friends can help me during this time by... _______________

____

____

What helps me remember you... _______________________________________

____

____

I'm really missing this about you... _______________________________________

____

Sometimes it feels like I'm the only one that remembers you; that makes me... _________

____

____

Every time is see/hear this: _______________________________ I think of you.

What I would tell you about my day... _______________________________

____

The hardest part of my day is... _______________________________

____

Today I'm really missing... _______________________________________

____

I find comfort when... _______________________________________

____

Date: ___ / ___ / ___

If I feel sad and need emotional support today, I will contact:

____

If you were here now... _______________________________

____

____

My first thoughts of today... _______________________

____

My school/teachers/friends can help me during this time by... _______________________

____

____

What helps me remember you... ____

____

____

I'm really missing this about you... _______________________________________

____

Sometimes it feels like I'm the only one that remembers you; that makes me... _______

____

____

Every time is see/hear this: _______________________________ I think of you.

What I would tell you about my day... _______________________________

____

The hardest part of my day is... _______________________________________

____

Today I'm really missing... _______________________________________

____

I find comfort when... _______________________________________

____

Date: /   /

If I feel sad and need emotional support today, I will contact:

____

If you were here now... _______________________________

____

____

My first thoughts of today... _______________________

____

Today I:

☐ Feel neutral/okay

☐ Feel supported

☐ Feel brokenhearted

☐ Feel misunderstood

☐ Feel like crying

☐ Feel lonely

☐ Feel angry

☐ Feel tired

☐ Feel sad

My school/teachers/friends can help me during this time by... _______________________

____

____

What helps me remember you... _______________________________

____

____

I'm really missing this about you... _______________________________

____

Sometimes it feels like I'm the only one that remembers you; that makes me... ________

____

____

Every time is see/hear this: _______________________ I think of you.

What I would tell you about my day... _______________________

____

The hardest part of my day is... _______________________

____

Today I'm really missing... _______________________________

____

I find comfort when... _______________________________

____

Date: / /

If I feel sad and need emotional support today, I will contact:

____

If you were here now... _______________________

____

____

My first thoughts of today... _________________

My school/teachers/friends can help me during this time by... _______________________

____

____

What helps me remember you... ____

____

____

I'm really missing this about you... ____

____

Sometimes it feels like I'm the only one that remembers you; that makes me... _______

____

____

Every time is see/hear this: _________________________________ I think of you.

What I would tell you about my day... ____

____

The hardest part of my day is... ____

____

Today I'm really missing... ____

____

I find comfort when... ____

____

Date: /   /

If I feel sad and need emotional support today, I will contact:

____

If you were here now... ___________________________

____

____

My first thoughts of today... _______________________

____

My school/teachers/friends can help me during this time by... _______________

____

____

What helps me remember you... ____________________________________

____

____

I'm really missing this about you... ___________________________________

____

Sometimes it feels like I'm the only one that remembers you; that makes me... _______

____

____

Every time is see/hear this: _______________________________ I think of you.

What I would tell you about my day... _________________________________

____

The hardest part of my day is... ____________________________________

____

Today I'm really missing... _______________________________________

____

I find comfort when... ____

____

Date: /   /

If I feel sad and need emotional support today, I will contact:

____

If you were here now... _______________________________

____

____

My first thoughts of today... _________________________

____

My school/teachers/friends can help me during this time by... _______________________

____

____

What helps me remember you... _________________________________

____

____

I'm really missing this about you... ____________________________

____

Sometimes it feels like I'm the only one that remembers you; that makes me... ________

____

____

Every time is see/hear this: _______________________________ I think of you.

What I would tell you about my day... _______________________________

____

The hardest part of my day is... ___________________________

____

Today I'm really missing... ______________________________

____

I find comfort when... __________________________________

____

Date: _____ / _____ / _____

If I feel sad and need emotional support today, I will contact:

____

If you were here now... _______________________________

____

____

My first thoughts of today... _________________________

____

My school/teachers/friends can help me during this time by... _______________________

____

____

What helps me remember you... _______________________________________

____

____

I'm really missing this about you... _______________________________________

____

Sometimes it feels like I'm the only one that remembers you; that makes me... _________

____

____

Every time is see/hear this: _______________________________ I think of you.

What I would tell you about my day... _______________________________________

____

The hardest part of my day is... _______________________________________

____

Today I'm really missing... _______________________________________

____

I find comfort when... _______________________________________

____

Date: /   /

If I feel sad and need emotional support today, I will contact:

____

If you were here now... ___________________________

____

____

My first thoughts of today... ______________________

____

My school/teachers/friends can help me during this time by... ___________________

____

____

What helps me remember you... ___________________________________

____

____

I'm really missing this about you... _______________________________________

____

Sometimes it feels like I'm the only one that remembers you; that makes me... _________

____

____

Every time is see/hear this: ________________________________ I think of you.

What I would tell you about my day... _____________________________________

____

The hardest part of my day is... ____

____

Today I'm really missing... ____

____

I find comfort when... ____

____

If I feel sad and need emotional support today, I will contact:

____

If you were here now... _______________________________

____

____

My first thoughts of today... ____________________

My school/teachers/friends can help me during this time by... _______________________

____

____

What helps me remember you... _______________________________

____

____

I'm really missing this about you... _______________________________

____

Sometimes it feels like I'm the only one that remembers you; that makes me... _______

____

____

Every time is see/hear this: _______________________ I think of you.

What I would tell you about my day... _______________________________

____

The hardest part of my day is... _______________________________

____

Today I'm really missing... _______________________________

____

I find comfort when... _______________________________

____

Date: ___ / ___ / ___

If I feel sad and need emotional support today, I will contact:

____

If you were here now... _________________________________

____

____

My first thoughts of today... ____________________________

____

My school/teachers/friends can help me during this time by... ____________________

____

____

What helps me remember you... __________________________

____

____

I'm really missing this about you... _______________________

____

Sometimes it feels like I'm the only one that remembers you; that makes me... ________

____

____

Every time is see/hear this: _________________________________ I think of you.

What I would tell you about my day... _____________________

____

The hardest part of my day is... _________________________

____

Today I'm really missing... _____________________________

____

I find comfort when... _________________________________

____

Date: /   /

If I feel sad and need emotional support today, I will contact:

____

If you were here now... _______________________

____

____

My first thoughts of today... _________________

My school/teachers/friends can help me during this time by... _______________________

____

____

What helps me remember you... ____

____

____

I'm really missing this about you... ____

____

Sometimes it feels like I'm the only one that remembers you; that makes me... ________

____

____

Every time is see/hear this: ___________________________________ I think of you.

What I would tell you about my day... ____

____

The hardest part of my day is... ____

____

Today I'm really missing... ____

____

I find comfort when... ____

____

Date: / /

If I feel sad and need emotional support today, I will contact:

____

If you were here now... _______________________

____

____

My first thoughts of today... _______________________

____

My school/teachers/friends can help me during this time by... _______________________

____

____

What helps me remember you... _______________________________________

____

____

I'm really missing this about you... _______________________________________

____

Sometimes it feels like I'm the only one that remembers you; that makes me... _________

____

____

Every time is see/hear this: _______________________________ I think of you.

What I would tell you about my day... _______________________________

____

The hardest part of my day is... _______________________________

____

Today I'm really missing... _______________________________

____

I find comfort when... _______________________________

____

If I feel sad and need emotional support today, I will contact:

____

If you were here now... _______________________________

____

____

My first thoughts of today... ___________________________

____

My school/teachers/friends can help me during this time by... _______________________

____

____

What helps me remember you... ____

____

____

I'm really missing this about you... ____

____

Sometimes it feels like I'm the only one that remembers you; that makes me... _________

____

____

Every time is see/hear this: ______________________________________ I think of you.

What I would tell you about my day... ____

____

The hardest part of my day is... ____

____

Today I'm really missing... ____

____

I find comfort when... ____

____

Date: /   /

If I feel sad and need emotional support today, I will contact:

____

If you were here now... _________________________________

____

____

My first thoughts of today... ____________________________

____

My school/teachers/friends can help me during this time by... _______________________

____

____

What helps me remember you... ____________________________________

____

____

I'm really missing this about you... _________________________________

____

Sometimes it feels like I'm the only one that remembers you; that makes me... _______

____

____

Every time is see/hear this: ______________________________ I think of you.

What I would tell you about my day... _______________________________

____

The hardest part of my day is... ___________________________________

____

Today I'm really missing... ______________________________________

____

I find comfort when... ____

____

$Date:$ ___ / ___ / ___

If I feel sad and need emotional support today, I will contact:

____

If you were here now... _______________________________

____

____

My first thoughts of today... _______________________

____

My school/teachers/friends can help me during this time by... _______________

____

____

What helps me remember you... _________________________________

____

____

I'm really missing this about you... _________________________________

____

Sometimes it feels like I'm the only one that remembers you; that makes me... ________

____

____

Every time is see/hear this: _________________________ I think of you.

What I would tell you about my day... _________________________________

____

The hardest part of my day is... _________________________________

____

Today I'm really missing... _________________________________

____

I find comfort when... _________________________________

____

Date: /   /

If I feel sad and need emotional support today, I will contact:

____

If you were here now... _______________________

____

____

My first thoughts of today... __________________

____

My school/teachers/friends can help me during this time by... _______________________

____

____

What helps me remember you... _______________________________________

____

____

I'm really missing this about you... ____

____

Sometimes it feels like I'm the only one that remembers you; that makes me... ________

____

____

Every time is see/hear this: ___________________________________ I think of you.

What I would tell you about my day... _______________________________________

____

The hardest part of my day is... ____

____

Today I'm really missing... ____

____

I find comfort when... ____

____

Date: /   /

If I feel sad and need emotional support today, I will contact:

____

If you were here now... ____________________________

____

____

My first thoughts of today... ________________________

<table>
<tr><td>Today I:</td></tr>
<tr><td>☐ Feel neutral/okay</td></tr>
<tr><td>☐ Feel supported</td></tr>
<tr><td>☐ Feel brokenhearted</td></tr>
<tr><td>☐ Feel misunderstood</td></tr>
<tr><td>☐ Feel like crying</td></tr>
<tr><td>☐ Feel lonely</td></tr>
<tr><td>☐ Feel angry</td></tr>
<tr><td>☐ Feel tired</td></tr>
<tr><td>☐ Feel sad</td></tr>
</table>

My school/teachers/friends can help me during this time by... ____________________

____

____

What helps me remember you... ______________________________________

____

____

I'm really missing this about you... ___________________________________

____

Sometimes it feels like I'm the only one that remembers you; that makes me... _______

____

____

Every time is see/hear this: _________________________ I think of you.

What I would tell you about my day... ______________________________

____

The hardest part of my day is... ___________________________________

____

Today I'm really missing... ____

____

I find comfort when... ____

____

Date: /   /

If I feel sad and need emotional support today, I will contact:

____

If you were here now... _________________________________

____

____

My first thoughts of today... ____________________________

____

My school/teachers/friends can help me during this time by... _________________

____

____

What helps me remember you... _________________________________

____

____

I'm really missing this about you... _______________________________

____

Sometimes it feels like I'm the only one that remembers you; that makes me... ________

____

____

Every time is see/hear this: ___________________________________ I think of you.

What I would tell you about my day... _____________________________

____

The hardest part of my day is... ________________________________

____

Today I'm really missing... ____________________________________

____

I find comfort when... ____

____

If I feel sad and need emotional support today, I will contact:

____

If you were here now... _______________________

____

____

My first thoughts of today... ___________________

Today I:

☐ Feel neutral/okay
☐ Feel supported
☐ Feel brokenhearted
☐ Feel misunderstood
☐ Feel like crying
☐ Feel lonely
☐ Feel angry
☐ Feel tired
☐ Feel sad

My school/teachers/friends can help me during this time by... _______________

____

____

What helps me remember you... _________________________________

____

____

I'm really missing this about you... ______________________________

____

Sometimes it feels like I'm the only one that remembers you; that makes me... ________

____

____

Every time is see/hear this: ___________________________ I think of you.

What I would tell you about my day... ____________________________

____

The hardest part of my day is... _______________________________

____

Today I'm really missing... ___________________________________

____

I find comfort when... _______________________________________

____

Date: /   /

If I feel sad and need emotional support today, I will contact:

____

If you were here now... _______________________________

____

____

My first thoughts of today... ___________________________

____

My school/teachers/friends can help me during this time by... _______________

____

____

What helps me remember you... _________________________________

____

____

I'm really missing this about you... ______________________________

____

Sometimes it feels like I'm the only one that remembers you; that makes me... _______

____

____

Every time is see/hear this: ______________________________ I think of you.

What I would tell you about my day... ____________________________

____

The hardest part of my day is... _______________________________

____

Today I'm really missing... __________________________________

____

I find comfort when... _____________________________________

____

Date: /   /

If I feel sad and need emotional support today, I will contact:

____

If you were here now... ___________________________

____

____

My first thoughts of today... ______________________

____

My school/teachers/friends can help me during this time by... _______________________

____

____

What helps me remember you... ____

____

____

I'm really missing this about you... ____

____

Sometimes it feels like I'm the only one that remembers you; that makes me... _______

____

____

Every time is see/hear this: _______________________________ I think of you.

What I would tell you about my day... ____

____

The hardest part of my day is... ____

____

Today I'm really missing... ____

____

I find comfort when... ____

____

Date: __ / __ / __

If I feel sad and need emotional support today, I will contact:

____

If you were here now... _________________________

____

____

My first thoughts of today... ____________________

____

My school/teachers/friends can help me during this time by... _________________

____

____

What helps me remember you... __________________________________

____

____

I'm really missing this about you... _______________________________

____

Sometimes it feels like I'm the only one that remembers you; that makes me... ______

____

____

Every time is see/hear this: _________________________________ I think of you.

What I would tell you about my day... ____________________________

____

The hardest part of my day is... ________________________________

____

Today I'm really missing... ___________________________________

____

I find comfort when... _______________________________________

____

Date: / /

Today I:

☐ Feel neutral/okay

☐ Feel supported

☐ Feel brokenhearted

☐ Feel misunderstood

☐ Feel like crying

☐ Feel lonely

☐ Feel angry

☐ Feel tired

☐ Feel sad

If I feel sad and need emotional support today, I will contact:

____

If you were here now... ____________________________

____

____

My first thoughts of today... ____________________________

____

My school/teachers/friends can help me during this time by... ______________

____

____

What helps me remember you... ______________________________________

____

____

I'm really missing this about you... __________________________________

____

Sometimes it feels like I'm the only one that remembers you; that makes me... ________

____

____

Every time is see/hear this: ________________________________ I think of you.

What I would tell you about my day... ________________________________

____

The hardest part of my day is... ____________________________________

____

Today I'm really missing... ____

____

I find comfort when... ____

____

If I feel sad and need emotional support today, I will contact:

____

If you were here now... _______________________________

____

____

My first thoughts of today... _______________________

____

Today I:

☐ Feel neutral/okay
☐ Feel supported
☐ Feel brokenhearted
☐ Feel misunderstood
☐ Feel like crying
☐ Feel lonely
☐ Feel angry
☐ Feel tired
☐ Feel sad

My school/teachers/friends can help me during this time by... _______________________

____

____

What helps me remember you... _______________________________________

____

____

I'm really missing this about you... _______________________________________

____

Sometimes it feels like I'm the only one that remembers you; that makes me... _________

____

____

Every time is see/hear this: _______________________________ I think of you.

What I would tell you about my day... _______________________________________

____

The hardest part of my day is... _______________________________________

____

Today I'm really missing... _______________________________________

____

I find comfort when... _______________________________________

____

Date: ___ / ___ / ___

If I feel sad and need emotional support today, I will contact:

____

If you were here now... _________________________________

____

____

My first thoughts of today... _____________________________

____

My school/teachers/friends can help me during this time by... ________________

____

____

What helps me remember you... ___________________________________

____

____

I'm really missing this about you... ________________________________

____

Sometimes it feels like I'm the only one that remembers you; that makes me... ________

____

____

Every time is see/hear this: _______________________________ I think of you.

What I would tell you about my day... ______________________________

____

The hardest part of my day is... _________________________________

____

Today I'm really missing... ____________________________________

____

I find comfort when... _______________________________________

____

Date: /   /

If I feel sad and need emotional support today, I will contact:

____

If you were here now... _______________________________

____

____

My first thoughts of today... _______________________

Today I:

☐ Feel neutral/okay

☐ Feel supported

☐ Feel brokenhearted

☐ Feel misunderstood

☐ Feel like crying

☐ Feel lonely

☐ Feel angry

☐ Feel tired

☐ Feel sad

My school/teachers/friends can help me during this time by... _______________________

____

____

What helps me remember you... _______________________________

____

____

I'm really missing this about you... _______________________________

____

Sometimes it feels like I'm the only one that remembers you; that makes me... _______

____

____

Every time is see/hear this: _________________________________ I think of you.

What I would tell you about my day... _______________________________

____

The hardest part of my day is... _______________________________

____

Today I'm really missing... _______________________________

____

I find comfort when... _______________________________

____

Date: /   /

If I feel sad and need emotional support today, I will contact:

____

If you were here now... ___________________________

____

____

My first thoughts of today... _______________________

____

My school/teachers/friends can help me during this time by... _______________________

____

____

What helps me remember you... ____

____

____

I'm really missing this about you... ____

____

Sometimes it feels like I'm the only one that remembers you; that makes me... _______

____

____

Every time is see/hear this: _________________________________ I think of you.

What I would tell you about my day... _______________________________________

____

The hardest part of my day is... _______________________________________

____

Today I'm really missing... _______________________________________

____

I find comfort when... _______________________________________

____

If I feel sad and need emotional support today, I will contact:

____

If you were here now... _______________________________

____

____

My first thoughts of today... _________________________

____

Today I:

☐ Feel neutral/okay
☐ Feel supported
☐ Feel brokenhearted
☐ Feel misunderstood
☐ Feel like crying
☐ Feel lonely
☐ Feel angry
☐ Feel tired
☐ Feel sad

My school/teachers/friends can help me during this time by... ____________________

____

____

What helps me remember you... ____

____

____

I'm really missing this about you... _____________________________________

____

Sometimes it feels like I'm the only one that remembers you; that makes me... ________

____

____

Every time is see/hear this: ___________________________________ I think of you.

What I would tell you about my day... ____________________________________

____

The hardest part of my day is... _______________________________________

____

Today I'm really missing... ____

____

I find comfort when... ____

____

Date: / /

If I feel sad and need emotional support today, I will contact:

____

If you were here now... _________________________

____

____

My first thoughts of today... ____________________

<table>
<tr><td>Today I:</td></tr>
<tr><td>☐ Feel neutral/okay</td></tr>
<tr><td>☐ Feel supported</td></tr>
<tr><td>☐ Feel brokenhearted</td></tr>
<tr><td>☐ Feel misunderstood</td></tr>
<tr><td>☐ Feel like crying</td></tr>
<tr><td>☐ Feel lonely</td></tr>
<tr><td>☐ Feel angry</td></tr>
<tr><td>☐ Feel tired</td></tr>
<tr><td>☐ Feel sad</td></tr>
</table>

My school/teachers/friends can help me during this time by... _______________________

____

____

What helps me remember you... ____

____

____

I'm really missing this about you... ____

____

Sometimes it feels like I'm the only one that remembers you; that makes me... _________

____

____

Every time is see/hear this: _________________________________ I think of you.

What I would tell you about my day... ____

____

The hardest part of my day is... ____

____

Today I'm really missing... ____

____

I find comfort when... ____

____

If I feel sad and need emotional support today, I will contact:

____

If you were here now... _______________________________

____

____

My first thoughts of today... _______________________

____

My school/teachers/friends can help me during this time by... _______________________

____

____

What helps me remember you... ____

____

____

I'm really missing this about you... ____

____

Sometimes it feels like I'm the only one that remembers you; that makes me... _________

____

____

Every time is see/hear this: _______________________________ I think of you.

What I would tell you about my day... _______________________________________

____

The hardest part of my day is... ____

____

Today I'm really missing... ____

____

I find comfort when... ____

____

Date: ___ / ___ / ___

<table>
<tr><td>

If I feel sad and need emotional support today, I will contact:

____

If you were here now... _________________________

____

____

My first thoughts of today... ___________________

</td><td>

Today I:

☐ Feel neutral/okay
☐ Feel supported
☐ Feel brokenhearted
☐ Feel misunderstood
☐ Feel like crying
☐ Feel lonely
☐ Feel angry
☐ Feel tired
☐ Feel sad

</td></tr>
</table>

____

My school/teachers/friends can help me during this time by... _______________

____

____

What helps me remember you... _________________________________

____

____

I'm really missing this about you... _____________________________

____

Sometimes it feels like I'm the only one that remembers you; that makes me... _______

____

____

Every time is see/hear this: ____________________________ I think of you.

What I would tell you about my day... ___________________________

____

The hardest part of my day is... ________________________________

____

Today I'm really missing... ____________________________________

____

I find comfort when... ____

____

$\mathcal{D}ate$:   /   /

If I feel sad and need emotional support today, I will contact:

____

If you were here now... _________________________

____

____

My first thoughts of today... ___________________

____

<table>
<tr><td>Today I:</td></tr>
<tr><td>☐ Feel neutral/okay</td></tr>
<tr><td>☐ Feel supported</td></tr>
<tr><td>☐ Feel brokenhearted</td></tr>
<tr><td>☐ Feel misunderstood</td></tr>
<tr><td>☐ Feel like crying</td></tr>
<tr><td>☐ Feel lonely</td></tr>
<tr><td>☐ Feel angry</td></tr>
<tr><td>☐ Feel tired</td></tr>
<tr><td>☐ Feel sad</td></tr>
</table>

My school/teachers/friends can help me during this time by... _____________________

____

____

What helps me remember you... ____________________________________

____

____

I'm really missing this about you... _______________________________

____

Sometimes it feels like I'm the only one that remembers you; that makes me... ________

____

____

Every time is see/hear this: ____________________________ I think of you.

What I would tell you about my day... _______________________________

____

The hardest part of my day is... __________________________________

____

Today I'm really missing... ______________________________________

____

I find comfort when... ____

____

If I feel sad and need emotional support today, I will contact:

____

If you were here now... ______________________

____

____

My first thoughts of today... _________________

____

Today I:
- ☐ Feel neutral/okay
- ☐ Feel supported
- ☐ Feel brokenhearted
- ☐ Feel misunderstood
- ☐ Feel like crying
- ☐ Feel lonely
- ☐ Feel angry
- ☐ Feel tired
- ☐ Feel sad

My school/teachers/friends can help me during this time by... _______________

____

____

What helps me remember you... _________________________________

____

____

I'm really missing this about you... ______________________________

____

Sometimes it feels like I'm the only one that remembers you; that makes me... ________

____

____

Every time is see/hear this: _____________________________ I think of you.

What I would tell you about my day... _____________________________

____

The hardest part of my day is... _________________________________

____

Today I'm really missing... _____________________________________

____

I find comfort when... ____

____

Date: ___ / ___ / ___

If I feel sad and need emotional support today, I will contact:

____

If you were here now... _______________________________

____

____

My first thoughts of today... _______________________

____

My school/teachers/friends can help me during this time by... _______________________

____

____

What helps me remember you... _______________________________

____

____

I'm really missing this about you... _______________________________

____

Sometimes it feels like I'm the only one that remembers you; that makes me... _______

____

____

Every time is see/hear this: _______________________________ I think of you.

What I would tell you about my day... _______________________________

____

The hardest part of my day is... _______________________________

____

Today I'm really missing... _______________________________

____

I find comfort when... _______________________________

____

Date: / /

If I feel sad and need emotional support today, I will contact:

____

If you were here now... ________________________

____

____

My first thoughts of today... ___________________

____

My school/teachers/friends can help me during this time by... _______________________

____

____

What helps me remember you... ____

____

____

I'm really missing this about you... ____

____

Sometimes it feels like I'm the only one that remembers you; that makes me... _________

____

____

Every time is see/hear this: _____________________________________ I think of you.

What I would tell you about my day... ____

____

The hardest part of my day is... ____

____

Today I'm really missing... ____

____

I find comfort when... ____

____

Date: /   /

If I feel sad and need emotional support today, I will contact:

____

If you were here now... _______________________________

____

____

My first thoughts of today... _______________________

____

Today I:
☐ Feel neutral/okay
☐ Feel supported
☐ Feel brokenhearted
☐ Feel misunderstood
☐ Feel like crying
☐ Feel lonely
☐ Feel angry
☐ Feel tired
☐ Feel sad

My school/teachers/friends can help me during this time by... _______________________

____

____

What helps me remember you... _______________________________________

____

____

I'm really missing this about you... _______________________________________

____

Sometimes it feels like I'm the only one that remembers you; that makes me... _________

____

____

Every time is see/hear this: _______________________________ I think of you.

What I would tell you about my day... _______________________________________

____

The hardest part of my day is... _______________________________________

____

Today I'm really missing... _______________________________________

____

I find comfort when... _______________________________________

____

Date: /   /

If I feel sad and need emotional support today, I will contact:

____

If you were here now... _________________________

____

____

My first thoughts of today... ____________________

____

My school/teachers/friends can help me during this time by... _________________

____

____

What helps me remember you... ____

____

____

I'm really missing this about you... _______________________________________

____

Sometimes it feels like I'm the only one that remembers you; that makes me... ________

____

____

Every time is see/hear this: ________________________________ I think of you.

What I would tell you about my day... ____________________________________

____

The hardest part of my day is... ____

____

Today I'm really missing... ____

____

I find comfort when... ____

____

Date: /   /

If I feel sad and need emotional support today, I will contact:

____

If you were here now... _________________________

____

____

My first thoughts of today... ____________________

____

My school/teachers/friends can help me during this time by... _____________________

____

____

What helps me remember you... ____

____

____

I'm really missing this about you... ______________________________________

____

Sometimes it feels like I'm the only one that remembers you; that makes me... ________

____

____

Every time is see/hear this: ______________________________________ I think of you.

What I would tell you about my day... ____________________________________

____

The hardest part of my day is... ____

____

Today I'm really missing... ____

____

I find comfort when... ____

____

Date: / /

If I feel sad and need emotional support today, I will contact:

____

If you were here now... ________________________

____

____

My first thoughts of today... ___________________

____

My school/teachers/friends can help me during this time by... _______________________

____

____

What helps me remember you... ____

____

____

I'm really missing this about you... ____

____

Sometimes it feels like I'm the only one that remembers you; that makes me... _________

____

____

Every time is see/hear this: _____________________________________ I think of you.

What I would tell you about my day... ____

____

The hardest part of my day is... ____

____

Today I'm really missing... ____

____

I find comfort when... ____

____

Date: /   /

If I feel sad and need emotional support today, I will contact:

____

If you were here now... _______________________________

____

____

My first thoughts of today... _______________________

My school/teachers/friends can help me during this time by... _______________________

____

____

What helps me remember you... _______________________________

____

____

I'm really missing this about you... _______________________________

____

Sometimes it feels like I'm the only one that remembers you; that makes me... _________

____

____

Every time is see/hear this: _________________________________ I think of you.

What I would tell you about my day... _______________________________

____

The hardest part of my day is... _______________________________

____

Today I'm really missing... _______________________________

____

I find comfort when... _______________________________

____

If I feel sad and need emotional support today, I will contact:

____

If you were here now... _______________________

____

____

My first thoughts of today... _________________

____

Today I:

☐ Feel neutral/okay
☐ Feel supported
☐ Feel brokenhearted
☐ Feel misunderstood
☐ Feel like crying
☐ Feel lonely
☐ Feel angry
☐ Feel tired
☐ Feel sad

My school/teachers/friends can help me during this time by... ______________________

____

____

What helps me remember you... ____

____

____

I'm really missing this about you... ___________________________________

____

Sometimes it feels like I'm the only one that remembers you; that makes me... ________

____

____

Every time is see/hear this: ____________________________________ I think of you.

What I would tell you about my day... __________________________________

____

The hardest part of my day is... _______________________________________

____

Today I'm really missing... ____

____

I find comfort when... ____

____

Date: /   /

If I feel sad and need emotional support today, I will contact:

____

If you were here now... _________________________________

____

____

My first thoughts of today... ____________________________

____

My school/teachers/friends can help me during this time by... ________________

____

____

What helps me remember you... __________________________________

____

____

I'm really missing this about you... ________________________________

____

Sometimes it feels like I'm the only one that remembers you; that makes me... ________

____

____

Every time is see/hear this: _________________________________ I think of you.

What I would tell you about my day... _______________________________

____

The hardest part of my day is... ___________________________________

____

Today I'm really missing... ______________________________________

____

I find comfort when... ____

____

Date: ___/___/___

If I feel sad and need emotional support today, I will contact:

____

If you were here now... ___________________________

____

____

My first thoughts of today... ______________________

____

My school/teachers/friends can help me during this time by... ___________________

____

____

What helps me remember you... ____________________

____

____

I'm really missing this about you... _________________

____

Sometimes it feels like I'm the only one that remembers you; that makes me... ________

____

____

Every time is see/hear this: _____________________ I think of you.

What I would tell you about my day... _______________

____

The hardest part of my day is... ___________________

____

Today I'm really missing... _______________________

____

I find comfort when... ____________________________

____

Date: / /

If I feel sad and need emotional support today, I will contact:

____

If you were here now... ______________________________

____

____

My first thoughts of today... ___________________________

____

My school/teachers/friends can help me during this time by... __________________

____

____

What helps me remember you... _________________________________

____

____

I'm really missing this about you... _______________________________

____

Sometimes it feels like I'm the only one that remembers you; that makes me... ________

____

____

Every time is see/hear this: ____________________________ I think of you.

What I would tell you about my day... _____________________________

____

The hardest part of my day is... ________________________________

____

Today I'm really missing... ___________________________________

____

I find comfort when... _______________________________________

____

Date: /   /

If I feel sad and need emotional support today, I will contact:

____

If you were here now... _________________________

____

____

My first thoughts of today... ____________________

____

My school/teachers/friends can help me during this time by... _______________

____

____

What helps me remember you... _____________________________________

____

____

I'm really missing this about you... __________________________________

____

Sometimes it feels like I'm the only one that remembers you; that makes me... _______

____

____

Every time is see/hear this: _________________________________ I think of you.

What I would tell you about my day... _________________________________

____

The hardest part of my day is... _____________________________________

____

Today I'm really missing... ____

____

I find comfort when... ____

____

Date: / /

If I feel sad and need emotional support today, I will contact:

____

If you were here now... ___________________________

____

____

My first thoughts of today... ______________________

____

My school/teachers/friends can help me during this time by... _______________________

____

____

What helps me remember you... ____

____

____

I'm really missing this about you... ____

____

Sometimes it feels like I'm the only one that remembers you; that makes me... ________

____

____

Every time is see/hear this: _____________________________________ I think of you.

What I would tell you about my day... ____

____

The hardest part of my day is... ____

____

Today I'm really missing... ____

____

I find comfort when... ____

____

Date: /   /

If I feel sad and need emotional support today, I will contact:

____

If you were here now... _______________________

____

____

My first thoughts of today... __________________

____

My school/teachers/friends can help me during this time by... _______________________

____

____

What helps me remember you... ____

____

____

I'm really missing this about you... ____

____

Sometimes it feels like I'm the only one that remembers you; that makes me... ________

____

____

Every time is see/hear this: _______________________________________ I think of you.

What I would tell you about my day... ____

____

The hardest part of my day is... ____

____

Today I'm really missing... ____

____

I find comfort when... ____

____

Date: /   /

If I feel sad and need emotional support today, I will contact:

____

If you were here now... _______________________________

____

____

My first thoughts of today... __________________________

____

My school/teachers/friends can help me during this time by... _______________

____

____

What helps me remember you... _________________________________

____

____

I'm really missing this about you... ______________________________

____

Sometimes it feels like I'm the only one that remembers you; that makes me... ________

____

____

Every time is see/hear this: _______________________________ I think of you.

What I would tell you about my day... _____________________________

____

The hardest part of my day is... ________________________________

____

Today I'm really missing... ___________________________________

____

I find comfort when... ______________________________________

____

Date: ___ / ___ / ___

If I feel sad and need emotional support today, I will contact:

____

If you were here now... _______________________________

____

____

My first thoughts of today... _______________________

____

My school/teachers/friends can help me during this time by... _______________

____

____

What helps me remember you... _______________________________

____

____

I'm really missing this about you... ____________________________

____

Sometimes it feels like I'm the only one that remembers you; that makes me... _______

____

____

Every time is see/hear this: _________________________ I think of you.

What I would tell you about my day... __________________________

____

The hardest part of my day is... ______________________________

____

Today I'm really missing... _________________________________

____

I find comfort when... _____________________________________

____

Date: /   /

If I feel sad and need emotional support today, I will contact:

____

If you were here now... _______________________

____

____

My first thoughts of today... _________________

____

My school/teachers/friends can help me during this time by... _______________________

____

____

What helps me remember you... ____

____

____

I'm really missing this about you... ____

____

Sometimes it feels like I'm the only one that remembers you; that makes me... ________

____

____

Every time is see/hear this: _________________________________ I think of you.

What I would tell you about my day... ____

____

The hardest part of my day is... ____

____

Today I'm really missing... ____

____

I find comfort when... ____

____

Date: / /

If I feel sad and need emotional support today, I will contact:

____

If you were here now... _______________________

____

____

My first thoughts of today... _________________

____

My school/teachers/friends can help me during this time by... _______________________

____

____

What helps me remember you... ____

____

____

I'm really missing this about you... ____

____

Sometimes it feels like I'm the only one that remembers you; that makes me... _________

____

____

Every time is see/hear this: _________________________________ I think of you.

What I would tell you about my day... ____

____

The hardest part of my day is... ____

____

Today I'm really missing... ____

____

I find comfort when... ____

____

Date: /   /

If I feel sad and need emotional support today, I will contact:

____

If you were here now... _______________________________

____

____

My first thoughts of today... _________________________

My school/teachers/friends can help me during this time by... _______________________

____

____

What helps me remember you... _______________________________________

____

____

I'm really missing this about you... ____________________________________

____

Sometimes it feels like I'm the only one that remembers you; that makes me... _________

____

____

Every time is see/hear this: ___________________________________ I think of you.

What I would tell you about my day... ___________________________________

____

The hardest part of my day is... _______________________________________

____

Today I'm really missing... ____

____

I find comfort when... ____

____

Date: /   /

If I feel sad and need emotional support today, I will contact:

____

If you were here now... _________________________

____

____

My first thoughts of today... ____________________

____

My school/teachers/friends can help me during this time by... _______________________

____

____

What helps me remember you... ____

____

____

I'm really missing this about you... ______________________________________

____

Sometimes it feels like I'm the only one that remembers you; that makes me... _______

____

____

Every time is see/hear this: _________________________________ I think of you.

What I would tell you about my day... ____________________________________

____

The hardest part of my day is... ____

____

Today I'm really missing... ____

____

I find comfort when... ____

____

Date: / /

If I feel sad and need emotional support today, I will contact:

____

If you were here now... _______________________________

____

____

My first thoughts of today... _______________________________

____

My school/teachers/friends can help me during this time by... _______________________________

____

____

What helps me remember you... _______________________________

____

____

I'm really missing this about you... _______________________________

____

Sometimes it feels like I'm the only one that remembers you; that makes me... _______________________________

____

____

Every time is see/hear this: _______________________________ I think of you.

What I would tell you about my day... _______________________________

____

The hardest part of my day is... _______________________________

____

Today I'm really missing... _______________________________

____

I find comfort when... _______________________________

____

Date: / /

If I feel sad and need emotional support today, I will contact:

____

If you were here now... _________________________

____

____

My first thoughts of today... ____________________

____

My school/teachers/friends can help me during this time by... _______________

____

____

What helps me remember you... _________________________________

____

____

I'm really missing this about you... _________________________________

____

Sometimes it feels like I'm the only one that remembers you; that makes me... _______

____

____

Every time is see/hear this: _________________________ I think of you.

What I would tell you about my day... _________________________________

____

The hardest part of my day is... _________________________________

____

Today I'm really missing... _________________________________

____

I find comfort when... _________________________________

____

$Date$: ______ / ______ / ______

If I feel sad and need emotional support today, I will contact:

____

If you were here now... _______________________

____

____

My first thoughts of today... _________________

____

<table>
<tr><td>Today I:</td></tr>
<tr><td>☐ Feel neutral/okay</td></tr>
<tr><td>☐ Feel supported</td></tr>
<tr><td>☐ Feel brokenhearted</td></tr>
<tr><td>☐ Feel misunderstood</td></tr>
<tr><td>☐ Feel like crying</td></tr>
<tr><td>☐ Feel lonely</td></tr>
<tr><td>☐ Feel angry</td></tr>
<tr><td>☐ Feel tired</td></tr>
<tr><td>☐ Feel sad</td></tr>
</table>

My school/teachers/friends can help me during this time by... _______________________

____

____

What helps me remember you... ____

____

____

I'm really missing this about you... _____________________________________

____

Sometimes it feels like I'm the only one that remembers you; that makes me... _______

____

____

Every time is see/hear this: ____________________________ I think of you.

What I would tell you about my day... ___________________________________

____

The hardest part of my day is... ____

____

Today I'm really missing... ____

____

I find comfort when... ____

____

Date: / /

If I feel sad and need emotional support today, I will contact:

____

If you were here now... _____________________________

____

____

My first thoughts of today... _______________________

My school/teachers/friends can help me during this time by... _____________________

____

____

What helps me remember you... _________________________________

____

____

I'm really missing this about you... _______________________________

____

Sometimes it feels like I'm the only one that remembers you; that makes me... ________

____

____

Every time is see/hear this: _______________________________ I think of you.

What I would tell you about my day... ______________________________

____

The hardest part of my day is... __________________________________

____

Today I'm really missing... _____________________________________

____

I find comfort when... ____

____

Date: ___/___/___

If I feel sad and need emotional support today, I will contact:

____

If you were here now... _________________________

____

____

My first thoughts of today... ____________________

____

My school/teachers/friends can help me during this time by... _______________________

____

____

What helps me remember you... ____

____

____

I'm really missing this about you... ____

____

Sometimes it feels like I'm the only one that remembers you; that makes me... ________

____

____

Every time is see/hear this: _________________________________ I think of you.

What I would tell you about my day... ______________________________________

____

The hardest part of my day is... ____

____

Today I'm really missing... ____

____

I find comfort when... ____

____

$\mathcal{D}$ate: /   /

If I feel sad and need emotional support today, I will contact:

____

If you were here now... _________________________________

____

____

My first thoughts of today... ____________________________

____

<table>
<tr><td>Today I:</td></tr>
<tr><td>☐ Feel neutral/okay</td></tr>
<tr><td>☐ Feel supported</td></tr>
<tr><td>☐ Feel brokenhearted</td></tr>
<tr><td>☐ Feel misunderstood</td></tr>
<tr><td>☐ Feel like crying</td></tr>
<tr><td>☐ Feel lonely</td></tr>
<tr><td>☐ Feel angry</td></tr>
<tr><td>☐ Feel tired</td></tr>
<tr><td>☐ Feel sad</td></tr>
</table>

My school/teachers/friends can help me during this time by... _______________

____

____

What helps me remember you... __________________________________

____

____

I'm really missing this about you... ______________________________

____

Sometimes it feels like I'm the only one that remembers you; that makes me... ________

____

____

Every time is see/hear this: _________________________________ I think of you.

What I would tell you about my day... _____________________________

____

The hardest part of my day is... ________________________________

____

Today I'm really missing... ___________________________________

____

I find comfort when... _______________________________________

____

Date: / /

If I feel sad and need emotional support today, I will contact:

____

If you were here now... _______________________________

____

____

My first thoughts of today... _______________________

____

My school/teachers/friends can help me during this time by... _______________

____

____

What helps me remember you... ___________________________________

____

____

I'm really missing this about you... _________________________________

____

Sometimes it feels like I'm the only one that remembers you; that makes me... ________

____

____

Every time is see/hear this: _______________________________ I think of you.

What I would tell you about my day... _______________________________

____

The hardest part of my day is... ___________________________________

____

Today I'm really missing... _______________________________________

____

I find comfort when... ____

____

Date: /   /

If I feel sad and need emotional support today, I will contact:

____

If you were here now... _______________________________

____

____

My first thoughts of today... ___________________________

____

<table>
<tr><td>

Today I:

☐ Feel neutral/okay

☐ Feel supported

☐ Feel brokenhearted

☐ Feel misunderstood

☐ Feel like crying

☐ Feel lonely

☐ Feel angry

☐ Feel tired

☐ Feel sad

</td></tr>
</table>

My school/teachers/friends can help me during this time by... __________________

____

____

What helps me remember you... _________________________________

____

____

I'm really missing this about you... ______________________________

____

Sometimes it feels like I'm the only one that remembers you; that makes me... ________

____

____

Every time is see/hear this: _________________________ I think of you.

What I would tell you about my day... _____________________________

____

The hardest part of my day is... _______________________________

____

Today I'm really missing... __________________________________

____

I find comfort when... ____________________________________

____

Date: / /

If I feel sad and need emotional support today, I will contact:

____

If you were here now... _______________________

____

____

My first thoughts of today... _________________

____

My school/teachers/friends can help me during this time by... _______________

____

____

What helps me remember you... __________________________________

____

____

I'm really missing this about you... ____________________________

____

Sometimes it feels like I'm the only one that remembers you; that makes me... ________

____

____

Every time is see/hear this: _________________________________ I think of you.

What I would tell you about my day... ___________________________

____

The hardest part of my day is... _______________________________

____

Today I'm really missing... ___________________________________

____

I find comfort when... _______________________________________

____

Today I:

☐ Feel neutral/okay
☐ Feel supported
☐ Feel brokenhearted
☐ Feel misunderstood
☐ Feel like crying
☐ Feel lonely
☐ Feel angry
☐ Feel tired
☐ Feel sad

Date: _____ / _____ / _____

If I feel sad and need emotional support today, I will contact:

____

If you were here now... _______________________________

____

____

My first thoughts of today... _______________________

____

My school/teachers/friends can help me during this time by... _______________

____

____

What helps me remember you... _______________________________

____

____

I'm really missing this about you... _______________________________

____

Sometimes it feels like I'm the only one that remembers you; that makes me... _________

____

____

Every time is see/hear this: _________________________________ I think of you.

What I would tell you about my day... _______________________________

____

The hardest part of my day is... _______________________________

____

Today I'm really missing... _______________________________

____

I find comfort when... _______________________________

____

Date: / /

If I feel sad and need emotional support today, I will contact:

____

If you were here now... ________________________________

____

____

My first thoughts of today... __________________________

____

My school/teachers/friends can help me during this time by... _______________________

____

____

What helps me remember you... ____

____

____

I'm really missing this about you... ____

____

Sometimes it feels like I'm the only one that remembers you; that makes me... ________

____

____

Every time is see/hear this: ___________________________________ I think of you.

What I would tell you about my day... ____

____

The hardest part of my day is... ____

____

Today I'm really missing... ____

____

I find comfort when... ____

____

Date: ___ / ___ / ___

Today I:

☐ Feel neutral/okay
☐ Feel supported
☐ Feel brokenhearted
☐ Feel misunderstood
☐ Feel like crying
☐ Feel lonely
☐ Feel angry
☐ Feel tired
☐ Feel sad

If I feel sad and need emotional support today, I will contact:

____

If you were here now... ______________________________

____

____

My first thoughts of today... _______________________

____

My school/teachers/friends can help me during this time by... ______________________

____

____

What helps me remember you... ____

____

____

I'm really missing this about you... ____

____

Sometimes it feels like I'm the only one that remembers you; that makes me... _________

____

____

Every time is see/hear this: _________________________________ I think of you.

What I would tell you about my day... ______________________________________

____

The hardest part of my day is... ______________________________________

____

Today I'm really missing... ______________________________________

____

I find comfort when... ______________________________________

____

Date: _____ / _____ / _____

If I feel sad and need emotional support today, I will contact:

____

If you were here now... _______________________________

____

____

My first thoughts of today... _______________________

____

My school/teachers/friends can help me during this time by... _______________________

____

____

What helps me remember you... _______________________________________

____

____

I'm really missing this about you... _______________________________________

____

Sometimes it feels like I'm the only one that remembers you; that makes me... _________

____

____

Every time is see/hear this: _________________________________ I think of you.

What I would tell you about my day... _______________________________________

____

The hardest part of my day is... _______________________________________

____

Today I'm really missing... _______________________________________

____

I find comfort when... _______________________________________

____

Date: ___ / ___ / ___

If I feel sad and need emotional support today, I will contact:

____

If you were here now... ______________________________

____

____

My first thoughts of today... ______________________

____

My school/teachers/friends can help me during this time by... _______________________

____

____

What helps me remember you... _______________________________

____

____

I'm really missing this about you... _______________________________

____

Sometimes it feels like I'm the only one that remembers you; that makes me... ________

____

____

Every time is see/hear this: _______________________________ I think of you.

What I would tell you about my day... _______________________________

____

The hardest part of my day is... _______________________________

____

Today I'm really missing... _______________________________

____

I find comfort when... _______________________________

____

If I feel sad and need emotional support today, I will contact:

____

If you were here now... _______________________________

____

____

My first thoughts of today... _______________________

____

My school/teachers/friends can help me during this time by... _______________________

____

____

What helps me remember you... _________________________________

____

____

I'm really missing this about you... _________________________________

____

Sometimes it feels like I'm the only one that remembers you; that makes me... _________

____

____

Every time is see/hear this: _________________________________ I think of you.

What I would tell you about my day... _________________________________

____

The hardest part of my day is... _________________________________

____

Today I'm really missing... _________________________________

____

I find comfort when... _________________________________

____

Date: /   /

If I feel sad and need emotional support today, I will contact:

____

If you were here now... _______________________________

____

____

My first thoughts of today... ____________________

<table>
<tr><td>Today I:</td></tr>
<tr><td>☐ Feel neutral/okay</td></tr>
<tr><td>☐ Feel supported</td></tr>
<tr><td>☐ Feel brokenhearted</td></tr>
<tr><td>☐ Feel misunderstood</td></tr>
<tr><td>☐ Feel like crying</td></tr>
<tr><td>☐ Feel lonely</td></tr>
<tr><td>☐ Feel angry</td></tr>
<tr><td>☐ Feel tired</td></tr>
<tr><td>☐ Feel sad</td></tr>
</table>

My school/teachers/friends can help me during this time by... _______________

____

____

What helps me remember you... _____________________________

____

____

I'm really missing this about you... _______________________________

____

Sometimes it feels like I'm the only one that remembers you; that makes me... ________

____

____

Every time is see/hear this: _________________________________ I think of you.

What I would tell you about my day... ________________________________

____

The hardest part of my day is... ___________________________________

____

Today I'm really missing... ___________________________________

____

I find comfort when... _______________________________________

____

Write Your Loved One A Letter

Use this space to write your loved one a personal letter. Think of everything you always wanted to say.

This Quote Makes Me Think Of You

Use this space to write a quote that makes you think of your loved one.

My Special Hashtags (#) When I Share Memories of You on Social Media

Use this space to create unique hashtags honoring your loved one on social media.

1. Talk about your loved one daily

2. Write down your thoughts about your loved one as they occur to you

3. Record your dreams about your departed loved one

4. Wear their favorite color

5. Dine at their favorite restaurant on a special occasion

6. Memorialize and update their social media pages

7. Create a memorial website with pictures and space for reflections from loved ones and friends

8. Plant a memorial tree

9. Organize a balloon release on special occasions

10. Visit their final resting spot frequently

11. Stay in contact with your loved one's closest friends and exchange memories

12. Create photo pillows and blankets with their image

13. Complete things they wanted to complete but they did not complete (I wrote and released a published book because my mom always wanted to be a published author)

14. Create and maintain a garden of their favorite fruits or vegetables

15. Honor their spirit during special occasions by placing a single rose in a chair honoring their spiritual presence

16. Celebrate /Acknowledge their heavenly birthdays

17. Commit Random Acts of Kindness

18. Create or join social media groups & exchange memories with others who have lost loved ones

19. Burn their favorite scented candles

20. Create a sacred box that includes precious items of your loved one

21. Name your child after your loved one

22. Go on a vacation that your loved one always wanted to go on

23. Walk on the beach barefoot and allow beautiful memories to flow about your loved one

24. Donate to their favorite charity/organization

25. Ask their favorite employer to create and hang a memorial plaque

26. Commit to adding different color bouquets every month at their gravesite

27. Care for their pet or adopt a pet in their honor

28. Speak of your loved one unapologetically

29. Wear jewelry that reminds you of your loved one (I wear bee jewelry to feel close to my mom's spirit since I always called her Miss Bee)

30. Say good morning to your loved one's spirit when you wake and goodnight at night

31. Play their favorite music, and dance while thinking happy memories.

List Additional Ways to Keep Your Loved One's Spirit Alive

____

____

____

____

____

____

There is no right or wrong way to honor your loved one's legacy or how to keep their spirit alive.

Whatever you do, don't abandon their spirit.

Kinyatta E. Gray is a motherless daughter, published author, and FlightsInStilettos Founder & CEO.

Website
https://www.flightsinstilettos.com/

Disclaimer: Kinyatta E. Gray is not a mental health provider and is providing this information based on real-life experience and to inspire others to keep their loved one's legacy alive. If you are experiencing a physical or emotional crisis, seek the help of a mental health professional.

OTHER GUIDED JOURNALS & DIARIES
by
KINYATTA E. GRAY

My Crazy Teenage Life

The Ultimate Expression Diary for Venting, Self-Reflections and Self-Love

---

Budget & Shop

A Monthly Personal Budget & Expense Tracker for Young Adults

Sweet Sixteen

Capturing Sweet Sixteen Moments & Memories

I miss you. I love you. I'm learning to live without you. I'm taking it day by day for as long as it takes.

Kinyatta E. Gray

AUTHOR & CELEBRITY TRAVEL INFLUENCER